Stakes

poems

by

Caitlin M.S. Buxbaum

Red Sweater Press
P.O. Box 870414
Wasilla, AK 99687
redsweaterpress.com

Copyright © 2019 Caitlin M.S. Buxbaum. All rights reserved.

No part of this book may be used or reproduced in any manner whatsoever without written permission of the publisher except in the case of brief quotations embodied in critical articles and reviews.

ISBN-13: 978-1-7332677-0-0
ISBN-10: 1-7332677-0-0

For the bold

Contents

I

Stakes	11
Codex	12
Stucco	13
Stress	14
Poet	15
Inspiration	16
A slumbering muse	17
Television	18
Generosity	19
Kismet	20
From	21
Plot	22

II

A different me	25
Editor / Good Enough	26
Girl in Dress, Walking Fast	27
Liar / The Human Condition	28
Weekend Warrior	29
Bibimbap	30
Head Cold / Termites	31
Procrastinating	32
Jealousy / Doubt	33
Why do you sit so small	34

III

April	37
Mother's Day Morning	38
Countdown	39
Grades	40
Inheritance	41

Middle School (69)	42
Silverware	43
Middle School (420)	44
The Seven	45
The Risks We Take	47

IV

Chappie	51
Numbers	53
Notre Dame	54
The Failure of Humanity / Roots	55
Waiting / Easter	56
Breath	57
Anger	58
Silence	59
Leaving	60
Resurrection	61
Transitions	62

Acknowledgments
About the Author

Stakes

I

Stakes
Codex
Stucco
Stress
Poet
Inspiration
A slumbering muse
Television
Generosity
Kismet
From
Plot

Stakes

If stakes were nought but wood which you
could hammer down or out, would you
worry you might become a liar,
false and filled with doubt?

Or would you let the flimsy fenceposts fly
and take the risk of living
a life of art and poverty,
beautiful, but unforgiving?

To hell with caution! The field is burning —
and would you know what else?
The tides of change are turning,
and your work is now your house!

Codex

Thumbing through the leaves of history,
my own or someone else's,
I see a pattern of marks on pages
that have tattooed a life of writing
on my soul — her soul, his —
an unending documentary
full of words meaning everything
and nothing.

What becomes of us when we die?
One can only hope
the letters of our lives
won't burn up
in the years that will forget us,
and will resurface
just in time.

Stucco

The texture of being held
and let go
over and over again,
each arm of the paint
pulled away
before it's ready to move on:
it's familiar

this ceiling style
reminds me of that unshakeable
restlessness so many leave
unaddressed — aren't we all
a little bit stuck
in our past lives, careers,
relationships?

But then, our struggles —
between what was
and what will be —
decorate the world,
in a more beautiful pattern
than we can see
on our own

Perhaps it's
where we're headed,
all along.

Stress

We're all stressed out
but we can't stress enough
how much we appreciate a friend's love,
or the perfectly metered stress
— unstressed/stressed —
of Shakespeare's sonnets.

We can say stress is distributed evenly
across a beam placed to support a home,
but ignore the way an earthquake or
reprimand, and the damage it causes,
can stress our minds & bodies…

When will we learn
from our own language
how to turn anxiety
into something that points positive,
instead of being made, by it,
into something stretched so thin
she hardly feels human?

Maybe one day, stress or no stress,
the words will come out right.

Poet

There are days when I
embrace the muse like a
best friend, and days
when it feels like a
clingy toddler, hanging
onto my pant leg, when
I'm just trying to play
the responsible adult, or
at least pretend this isn't
my lot in life, if only for
a moment's rest,
or indulgence
in worldly pleasures.

Inspiration

If a child asks,
'what is inspiration?'
what would you say?
It's a noun, but not
a person, place or thing,
because you can't see it, except
through the person who senses it,
and produces something from it;
it's like the Black Pearl's harbor —
none can find it, except for
those who already know
where it is. *The ship's real enough,
therefore its anchorage must be
a real place,* but inspiration —
and imagination, too —
transcend the real, blur
whatever line may be said
to exist between the real
and the unreal.

So what is inspiration?
Incomprehensible to those
who've never had it,
divine for those who have,
which is to say,
no less complex
or indescribable
for the inspired.

A slumbering muse

The quiet scream of the refrigerator
after an episode of *Supernatural*
and a book of Billy Collins poems
sets my heart and mind racing,
full of exhilarating and hysterical
possibility, until the sound turns
into an old modem, dialing up,
then dying away. Only then
am I able to put pen to paper,
to imagine what trivial things
can do for a slumbering muse.

Television

What is it that draws us
into a predictable, low-budget
television show, when we know
its cheap thrills and good-looking boys
(posing as men) are only as satisfying
as our temporary break from reality,
and the un-thought that it will come
crashing down on us, once again

I guess we all need to
feel a little love — a little fear —
loosely represented,
easily earned.

Generosity

Generosity is underrated —
whether it be of spirit
or in coin, though I'll take the former
if it means my heart
will last long enough
to motivate my mind
into believing in the Impossible,
into gaining the courage
to take a leap of faith
and trust my self
as much as I've deceived it;

if only life weren't dependent upon
that which costs, and sometimes
costs too much.

Kismet

It's curious that what could be
called kismet for one
could be "Greg" for another—that is,
where she feels fate, he senses
the complications
of believing it isn't just him
pulling the strings;
'one man's trash
is another man's treasure?' is that it?
one woman's dream
is another one's nightmare? is that it?

I only know that most things
aren't written in stone.

From

I am from here,
a home made from scraped knees
and a lack of good climbing trees,
summer lakes with leeches
and winter trails that keep us
busy during the long, cold, dark.

I am from there,
a place you've never been
but Would Like to Visit,
an aurora-rimmed wonderland
shining with possibility
and the promise of the PFD.

I am from nowhere,
the beautiful, brutal wasteland
where we practice "animal cruelty"
for sport, and addiction deaths
are matched only by suicides and SADness,
not to mention crimes of (teenage!) passion.

I am from Alaska.

Plot

What would happen if
there were no claims to stake
on the moon, or in
a vampire's heart? If there
were no ownership,
nor fear, nor lust?
A world such as this
has no pain, no mystery,
no plot to thicken—

and, after all,
who could you be,
without your own story?

II

A different me
Editor / Good Enough
Girl in Dress, Walking Fast
Liar / The Human Condition
Weekend Warrior
Bibimbap
Head Cold / Termites
Procrastinating
Jealousy / Doubt
Why do you sit so small

A different me

A mug from a man long past —
no, from a place that shares this man;
I've never been, so he's the one thing
we have in common.
Preparing my morning coffee,
I'm reminded of the quite literal
summer fling I always thought
I was too responsible to have,
and the mark it left on me — on him?
(Do I hope? Do I care?) It's this
thrift store purchase that has nothing
and everything to do with him,
however accidental,
that stirs me as I do my breakfast;
I know I make too much
of coincidental connections,
and though I'll often let them pass,
it won't mean I'll ever forget.

I can't imagine what it's like
to give yourself to so many someones,
so many times, over the course of a life,
when just one person's touch
seeps into my skin so deep,
I become a different me.

Editor / Good Enough

You send off your manuscript,
then think of all the things
that could go wrong:
a stilted stanza of dialogue,
a fragment you forgot to fix,
an emotional scene you planned
to eliminate later, but didn't,
or a typo you imagine will tip
the scales out of your favor,
and the editor will turn her back
on you, saying, *not good enough,*
and you'll internalize those words,
let them shape your belief in yourself

until the editor does email you back
and she says, *this needs work,*
but this is great! and you realize
all it takes to be "good enough"
is to believe you are, long enough
to make it through the waiting,
and stave off the nagging doubt.

Girl in Dress, Walking Fast

'Girl in Dress, Walking Fast'
is how the newspapers would know me
if only they'd ask, and interrupt
this broadcast of my life
to advertise my efficiency,
levied by the student-teacher-writer life
that leaves me less time to just be,
and more to be busy, without purpose.

Liar / The Human Condition

"How are you?" she asks,
and I wish she wouldn't,
because she doesn't want
the honest answer:
Terrible, no good, very bad...

because of things I did
and didn't do, some
in my control, and
many more beyond it,
or so it seems...

"Oh, not bad," I say,
"How are you?"

Weekend Warrior

There's something about Saturday
that shapes the world — the weekend —
as your oyster, open to all the wonderful
enjoyments in which you might partake,
spouting a seemingly unending steam
of carefree color…

But that Sunday, that deadline
before the day job, isn't as distant
as you think, and when it comes,
all those tasks you were sure
you had time to complete
seem impossible,
like insurmountable peaks of procrastination
maybe driving you to drink.

Bibimbap

You ordered it
with the special sauce,
of course you did —
to do otherwise would be
just shy of sacrilege.

About halfway through,
that's when the fire starts,
stinging your lips,
fingering its way around your mouth
and down your throat,
spilling out your nose,
burning your taste buds —
not quite to oblivion, but close —

and you've come this far,
so you might as well
finish it, even though
flavor has been displaced
by flames licking your tongue,
and gums, and belly…

in the end, was it worth it?
The meal gone in the snap
of its three syllables, you wonder
how you got here — full and on fire,
satisfied, yet wanting more.

Head Cold / Termites

Nothing like a bad head cold
to remind you of your own
mortality, that the sturdiest tree
can be felled by the tiniest bug,
like a flu virus, or a termite,
gnawing away inside until
survivor's doubt, not guilt, creeps in,
saying, *maybe it won't be alright*

and then the sickness passes,
and you realize you were
stronger than you thought.

Procrastinating

I 'can't avoid it anymore,'
you say,
but little do you know
how I have mastered
the art of getting by,
of losing myself
in a task so irrelevant
to the moment,
the impending deadline,
that I'll convince myself
— and you too —
that the thing about time
is its ability to bend a weak will
to work to your advantage.

Jealousy / Doubt

what gives you the right
to flaunt your so-called success
in the face of your clearer failures,
to use your own "tragedy"
to further your career?

Can she really be that good?

what makes you so special
that the shortcomings of you & yours
are allowed to take on lives of their own
and fund a lifestyle we all want,
but none of us deserve?

Is there any truth to her story?

what is it about me & mine
that's overshadowed by your
veneer of accomplishment, protected
from what people really think, say
about you, and what he's done?

Am I really so selfish?

how can any of us know
what our words are truly worth,
when our antagonism outweighs
our compassion & our acceptance
of what is, and what will
or may never be?

I guess we all should jump for a chance
to sit at the proverbial table.

Why do you sit so small

Why do you sit so small
in the earthen light,
shoulders hunched in fear
of what might not come,
or what breaking that line of thinking
could do to your reasoned existence?

Have faith, stand tall,
venture into the world of people
and places beyond the confines
of your mind, into the noise &
light pollution you *hate so much*,
if only to remember who you are,
where you began, and what life
awaits, outside your door

III

April
Mother's Day Morning
Countdown
Grades
Inheritance
Middle School (69)
Silverware
Middle School (420)
The Seven
The Risks We Take

April

April is like a month of Mondays:
From Fools Day on the first
to Tax Day on the fifteenth
(keep in mind we're only halfway
to the end now),
it spans the weeks without relief,
from the most irritating pranks
to the harshest realities of our lives —
which include the misleading promise
that *April showers bring May flowers*
(where are YOU from?) —
and that there's life after, not death,
but taxes, which haunt us like
irreverent ghosts of our financial failings,
or at least, some of our failures
to read and do math.

Mother's Day Morning

It's the *Far out!*
from the hungry homeless man
holding his "Happy Mother's Day"
sign at the railroad crossing
after I've given him some food
that has me thinking about
how easy it is to be kind,
and also how easy to be afraid,
and not move, for fear of what
we call The Unthinkable,
but have already thought
(don't we all have mothers?)

Ask yourself, then
what can you do, today?

Countdown

to a school year's closing,
and (maybe) the chapter of life;
to a journey abroad,
and the reminder of what we pray
hasn't been lost;
to the end of days,
an impending devastation that's
been a long time coming,
though we'll never be ready…

What's the point?

Maybe the simple marking of time
creates a rhythm in our souls
by which we're able to carry on,
to anticipate but not be weighed down
by that which looms ahead of us,
to say nothing of what's behind…

I suppose our fate is our own,
at least as we can picture it.

Grades

What is a grade, anyway,
when it comes to that kind of schooling
which everyone loves to complain about,
and demand be offered freely?
I think it's the one thing that matters most
for reasons it should matter least, and least
for reasons it should matter most.

Once, it was like a "call" home —
it was a display of achievement,
a ticket to ride, and now a label
students think they deserve,
no matter what they've done
or failed to do.

But of course, as my father says,
"until the pain of change is less
than that of staying the same,
the behavior remains," and
we tend not to do what is right,
but what is easy.

And don't say you're "sorry"
in order to excuse your laziness
or get the grade; remember,
an apology is only worth as much
as the change that follows it.

So, please: Look at your future,
and try again — *think* again, about
what a grade is, what a grade means,
and what grade your *work* merits.

Inheritance

Watching my handwriting morph
into a more muted methodical at
best, a sloppy smattering of slang
at worst, I imagine my capital As
and Ws, maybe my lowercase Ss,
merge with my father's; I wonder
in what other ways have I become
like him, what mannerisms and
modes of meaning do I construct
just the same as one that made me?
If an un-mimicked motion of the
hand can so momentously make
itself known so late in life, what
other matters might we inherit
from our mentors?

Middle School (69)

What is a pre-teen child,
that we can converse with it
like an adult, until they misunderstand
their place in the world, mistaking fairness
for equality, and measured interest
for whole-hearted support?

A child of this "middle" age
is even less comprehensible in action;
playful as a toddler, emotional on a level
far too advanced for the cause
of such distress. Yet their words
can hit us so hard, needling into us
without realizing the depth
of their accidental insight.

What are we to do,
when their height and
vocabulary suggest they might
be one of us, yet their attitudes and
humor — not always their naiveté —
show us just how young they are?

Silverware

after Billy Collins' "Divorce"

A clever comparison between
silverware & divorce has me
delighted, and also devastated
by the utter commonality of
such an offense; may we never
suffer the shimmering slights
of our imaginations.

Middle School (420)

it's the "threat of violence"
against our school
that has me thinking
of all the ticking time bombs
in the halls,
the students & teachers
who just might snap
if you flip that water bottle,
throw that pencil,
mention someone's "wenis"
one more time…

what would life be like
if everyone acted on their impulses,
did nothing they weren't forced to do,
said anything that came across their minds?
I think it would be called
Middle School,
and I shudder at the thought.

The Seven

It's a snowy, spring day and we seven
are pondering the gravity of the situation —
fifty percent of the student body gone,
for one reason or another, and we're still
breathing, but also wondering:

What could I have done?
What did I miss?
What needs aren't being met?

It's been a hell of a year, we've thought,
and where do we go from here?

Life goes on. Children may forget,
may still not know or understand,
but I can't help but think that we seven
are bound by what we didn't
or couldn't see, and what we know now;
what does this kind of failure say about us?
Are we marked by this in a way no one else is?
Why must we always go over this in our minds,
entertaining this nagging thought that
things could've played out differently?
They still might. Is there something about
this time of year, though? Or does
Columbine's anniversary have so much power?
Which is worse? A tragedy's influence
or a cosmic shift in the spring of student lives
that drives young minds to such madness?

Maybe dozens, even hundreds,
will remember this day, this week —
but will we seven forever bear
the invisible burden of having tried,

but not tried enough? Having seen,
but not seen enough? Of responsibility?
We may not be to blame, but we must be
united in our misery, and our moving on.

We are the seven.

The Risks We Take

It's the increase
in student resource officers
and airport security
that has me thinking about
the risks we take
simply by being
a student or a passenger,
someone hoping
to learn something,
to see something amazing
or at least worthwhile,
only sometimes realizing
who holds our lives
in their hands.

IV

Chappie
Numbers
Notre Dame
The Failure of Humanity / Roots
Waiting / Easter
Breath
Anger
Silence
Leaving
Resurrection
Transitions

Chappie

Cutting down a noose outside a church,
this Airborne Chaplain knows
what it means for Mosul,
but maybe not for the hundreds
watching, seeing the "throwback" photo
of a religious oppression ending,
or starting to end,
with the slice of a knife

Perhaps these hundreds
won't appreciate what the gesture cost,
what it took to reach that deadly strap,
limp in the leveled square, but
no less threatening

I bet he remembers more
than he wants to: Souls lost
and saved in the war for peace
that he often wonders why
he's fighting, even though
he believes it matters,
he matters,
He matters

but will he sleep again
without waking from visions
of death and destruction?
Is he shamed by what he didn't see,
more than what he didn't do?

Maybe he prays his faith won't be shaken,
but fears one last mortar blast
will do him in, just as he's
given up his God, almost by accident.

Perhaps his church is now his home, the
only place that feels safe
from unknowing eyes,
unsympathetic hearts.

God only knows
how his heart beats.

Numbers

Six million,
eight thousand,
eight hundred thousand —
numbers of lives (and loves) lost
in the greatest conflicts — genocides —
of the world, swept up in this thing called
History that shocks us, but also evades us
in our realities of Progress and ignorance;
we remember the numbers
as if that is the point

but perhaps those figures
are the only tethers to sanity we have
in the sea of senseless deaths
around the globe; maybe
the numbers are all we have
to measure just how
doomed we are

and find solace in the fact that we
have boxes to put our tragedies in.

Notre Dame

An electrical short circuit at Notre Dame
paid the world-renowned landmark in
charred interior, safety hazards, fragile walls
shored up with wooden planks of anonymity…

The fire was accidental. Some question Paris,
comment on whether a computer glitch or
the temporary elevators used in the
renovation work must be explored.

Vestiges dating from antiquity, under the
vast esplanade, restored Paris, with some saying,
thank the hundreds who battled the fast-moving fire,
preventing destruction and rescuing the right things.

The cathedral's soaring spire, organs,
were saved. For devotion, Paris—strung
from Victor Hugo—killed the blaze, the Seine
closed by risks and its centuries-old windows

who told the consecrated hosts that the
crown of thorns, Jesus at his crucifixion,
had already broken the protective covering
needed to finish the job, raise the extraordinary.

Humanity rages, steps up the spiral staircase;
you understood that it was really dramatic,
spreading quickly — it was a chance to
bounce back, to realize what unites us.

The Failure of Humanity / Roots

I have to wonder
reading Dallaire's account
of Easter around the Interahamwe
if Rwanda's "rich, red earth"
doesn't leech its color
from the blood of thousands
killed by incompetence
and devilish deals that
shocked the world too late—
what will we find when we
return to our roots? Will we
realize we were, and are,
the same? Let it be only
for the good of people,
not *the failure of humanity.*

Waiting / Easter

what's done in the waiting
They say
is as telling as the reaction
to the end of it,
positive or negative,
since your future is based
more on who you are
than who you could be,
and what you believe without seeing
than what you must see to believe

Breath

Look
closely
and you'll see
the constriction,
our breath held in by
the corset of our fears
and the world's expectations
squeezing our hearts so damn tightly
that all our 'inner beauty' floods out
just in time for eyes to open, and close.

Anger

Anger is as much about fear
as it is the boiling rage that
shudders through your entire being,
taking your breath away — fear that
whatever it is that brought you here
might actually be your fault.

Silence

Silence is not your friend
when the enemy appears
in the guise of kindness and
blows your dreams to bits—
it's the space in which you
go to die, and every harsh word
that's ever been said against you
is left ringing in your ears.

Leaving

whether it's a breakup
or the end of a bad job,
leaving is never easy;
you wonder what you did
to deserve the surprise
of realizing something
you'd thought was perfect
was never meant to be

Resurrection

there are days I wonder
if she can hammer the nail
in the coffin any harder
and then I remember that
with death comes new life
and I take 'courage, dear heart'
in the fact that I will not be
trapped by my misfortune
but be set free by my own
burial and resurrection

Transitions

A dream of a boy long gone,
now a man, has me thinking
about transitions, from one place
to another — in the physical,
as well as the emotional —
attachments waiting to be
severed, yet holding out hope
that one thing will change enough
to keep another from doing the same

it's times like these when I wonder
why I've made the choices I've made,
what would've happened if I had said
yes, let him lead me on into the unknown
I imagine would've ended in divorce

but it's that memory of fondness
that puts a smile on my face, and
a watermark of happiness on the past,
while I know full well those years
will never be remade, nor erased.

–|||▮|||–

Acknowledgments

Thank you to my good friend and fellow Gustie, Rebecca Hare, who provided valuable feedback on the first and second drafts of these poems.

Thank you to my students and co-workers who inspired and supported me during my first year teaching. To those who contributed to the struggles, know that something good came of it, and if nothing else, you can take pride in that.

And thank you always to the poets & writers & readers of the world — with you, anything is possible.

About the Author

Caitlin M.S. Buxbaum is a poet, novelist and former journalist from Wasilla, Alaska. She has a Master of Arts in Teaching from the University of Alaska Anchorage and a Bachelor of Arts in Japanese and English with an emphasis in Creative Writing from Gustavus Adolphus College.

Other Books by Caitlin M.S. Buxbaum

The Compendium of Lost Poems
Uneven Lanes
Wabi-Sabi World: An Artist's Search
Ever Unknown, Ever Misunderstood
Songs from the Underground

Follow the author on Facebook, Twitter & Instagram @caitbuxbaum
or visit her website: caitbuxbaum.com

www.ingramcontent.com/pod-product-compliance
Lightning Source LLC
Chambersburg PA
CBHW060217050426
42446CB00013B/3100